I0485629

Dogs Coloring Book For Adults

BIG DOGS

Fantasy Art Coloring Book For Stress Relief

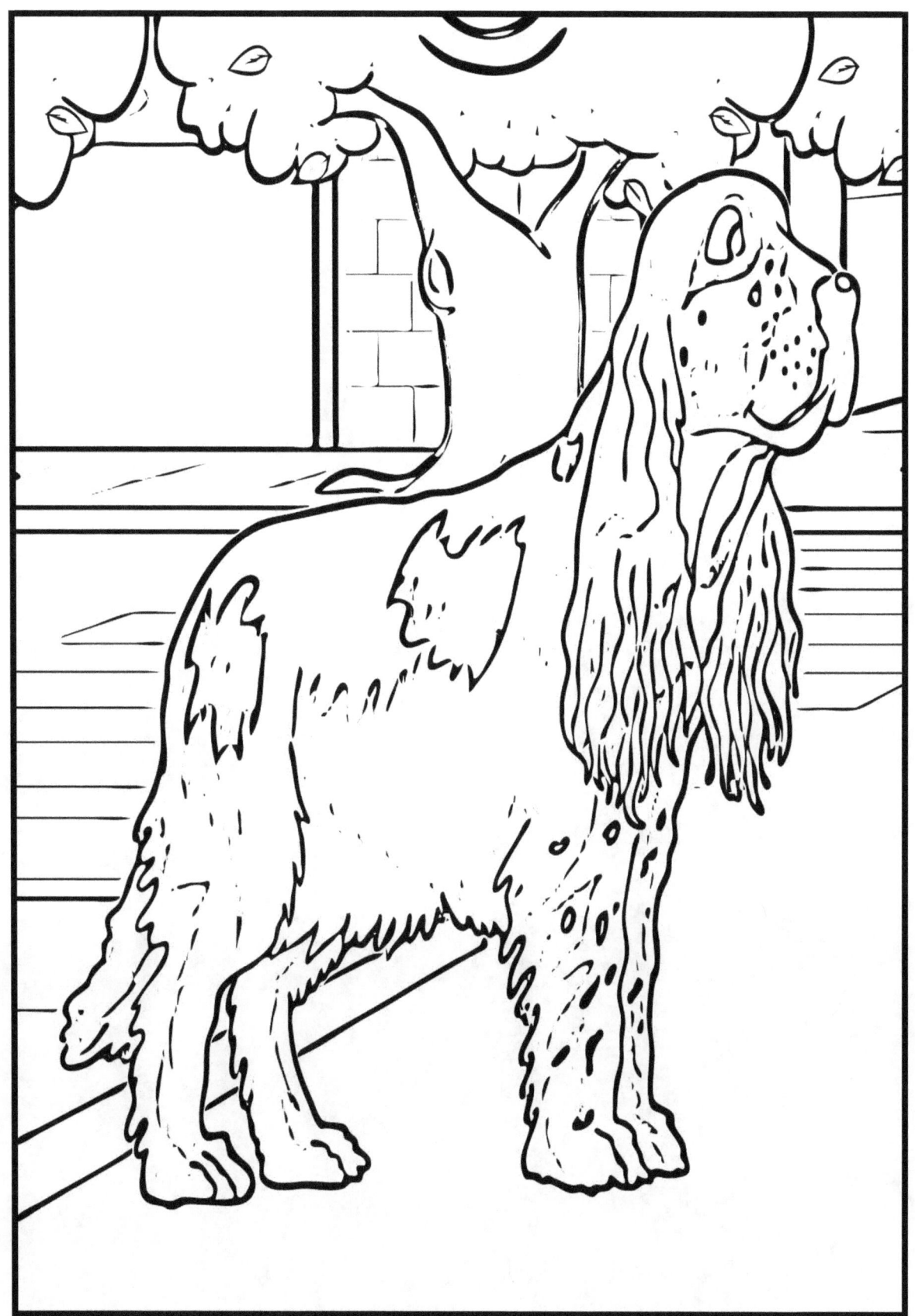

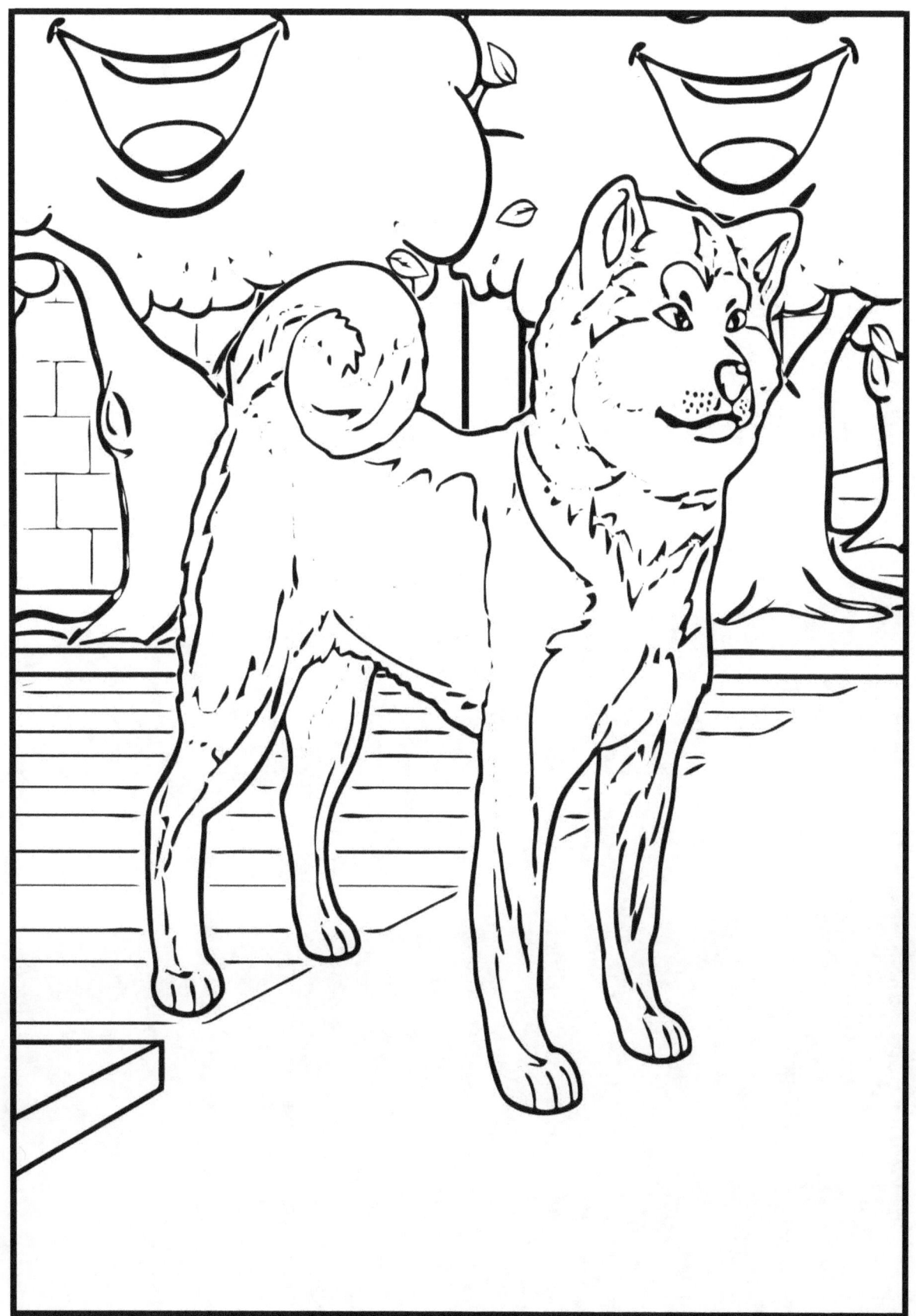

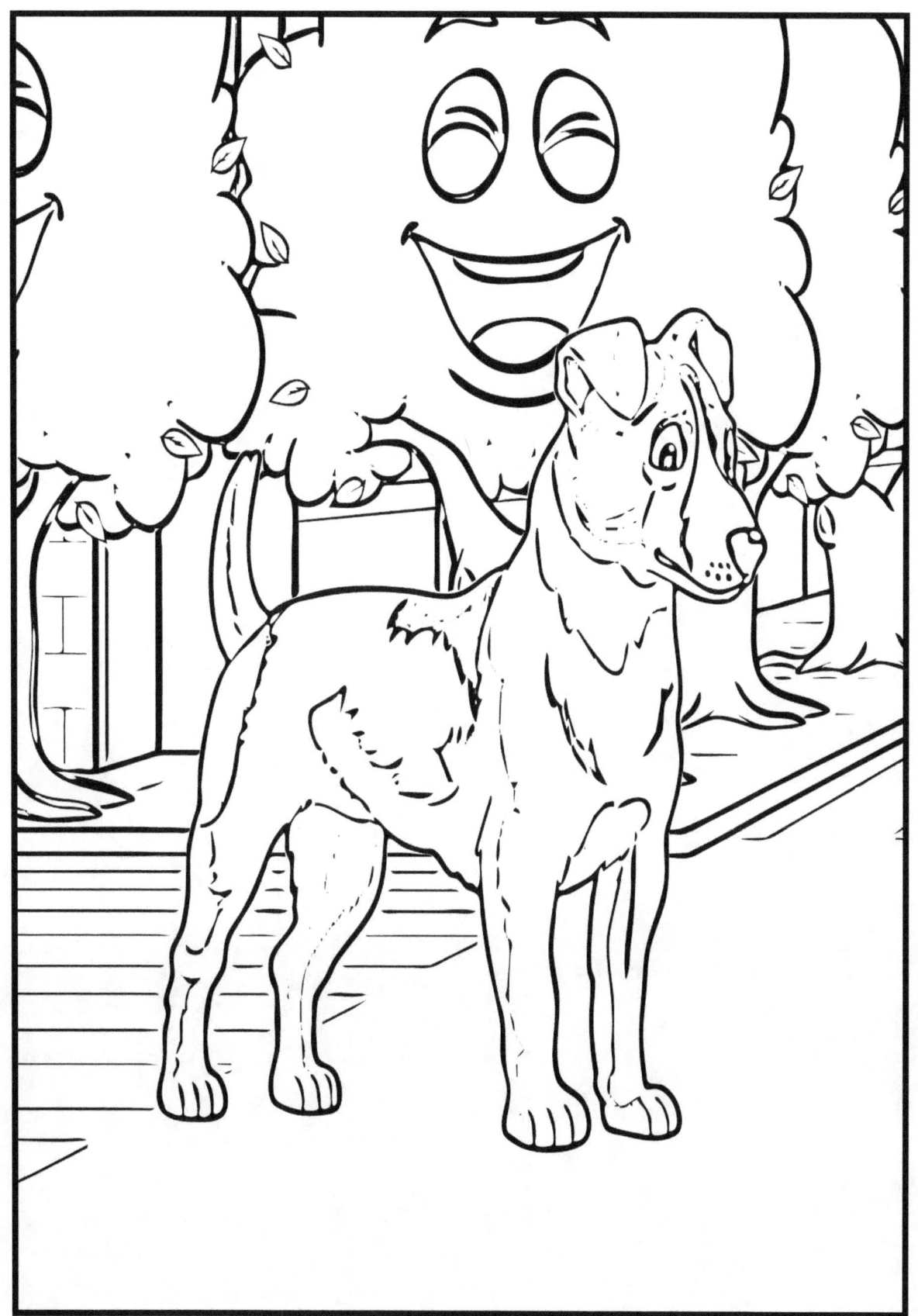

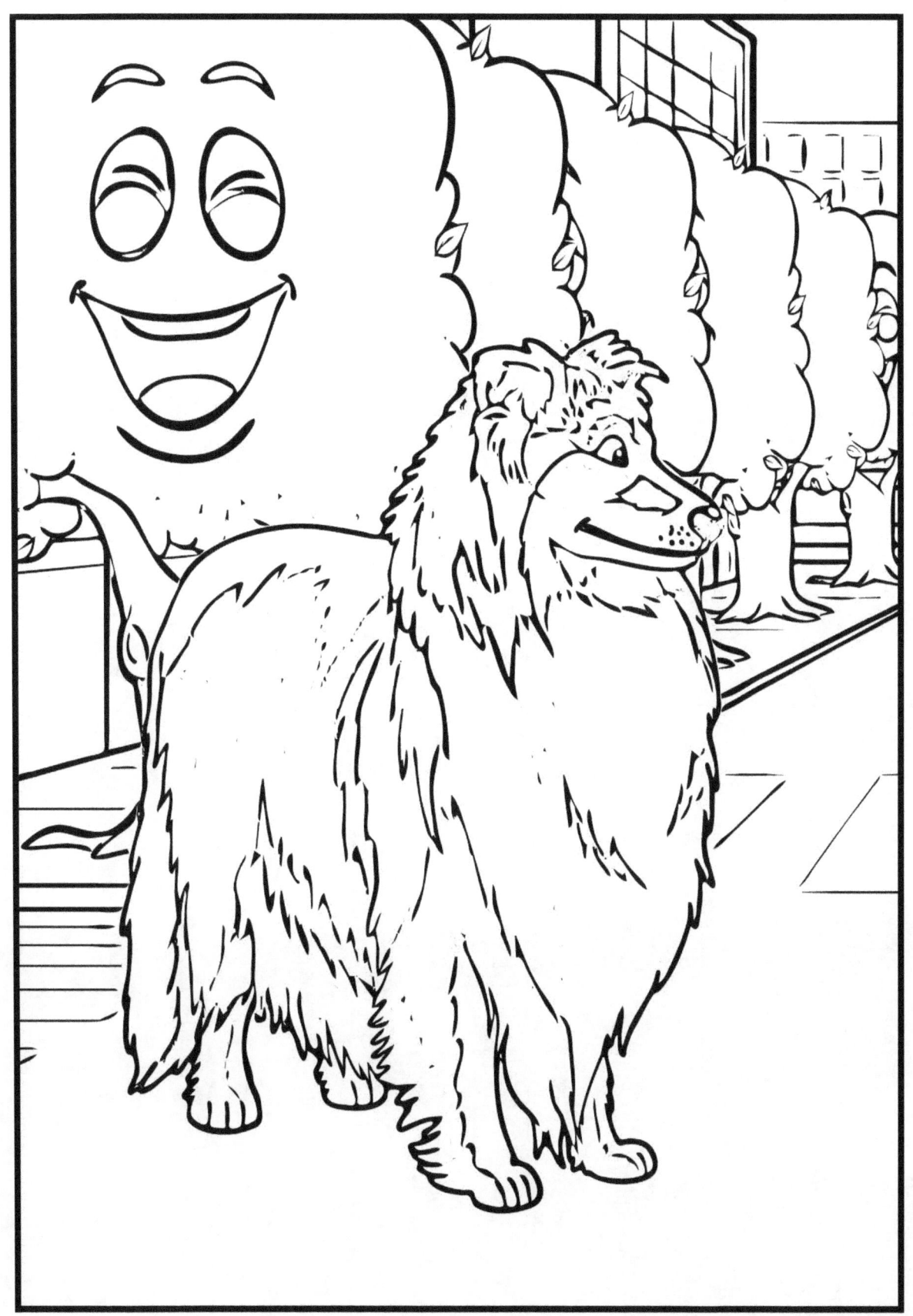

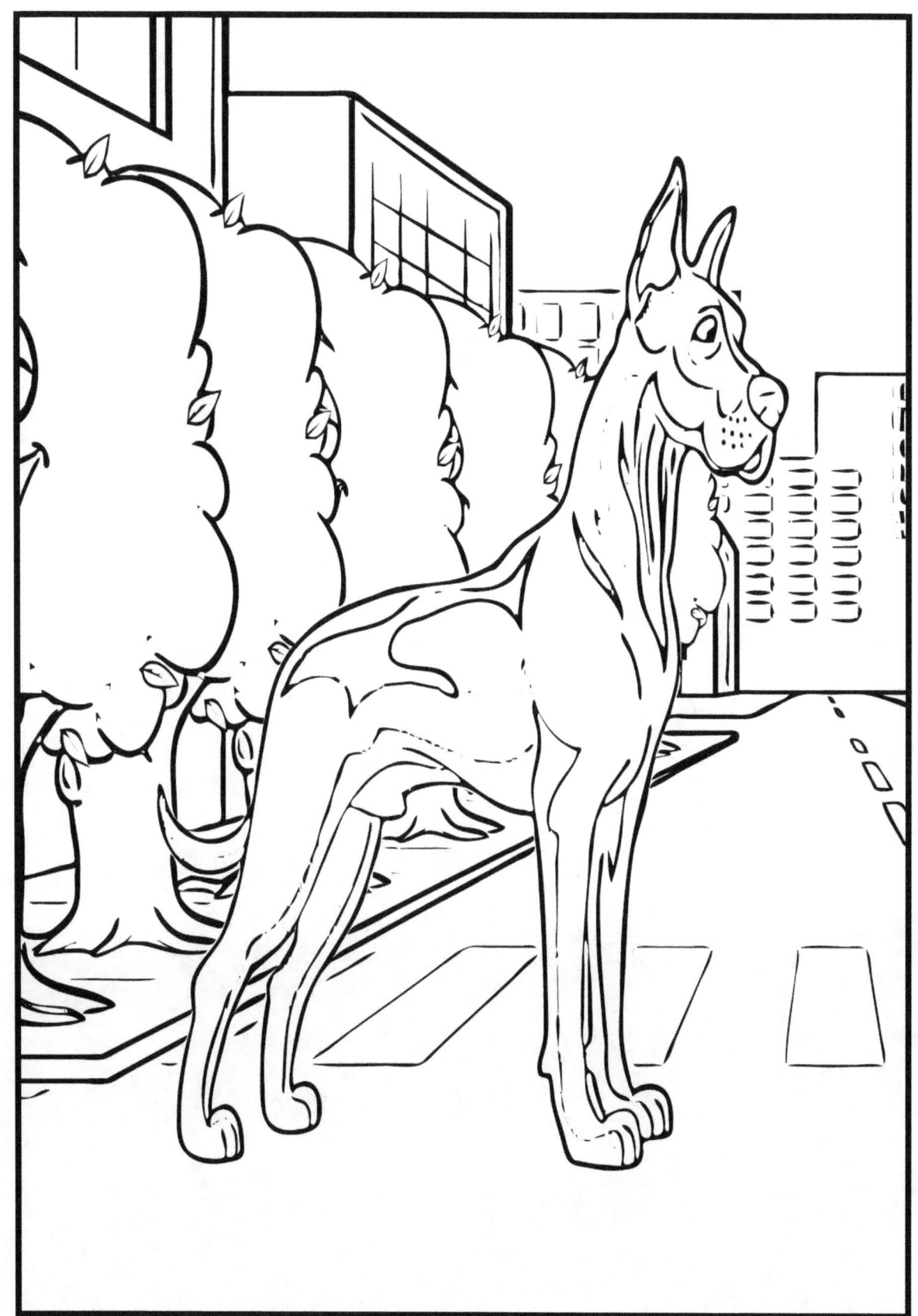

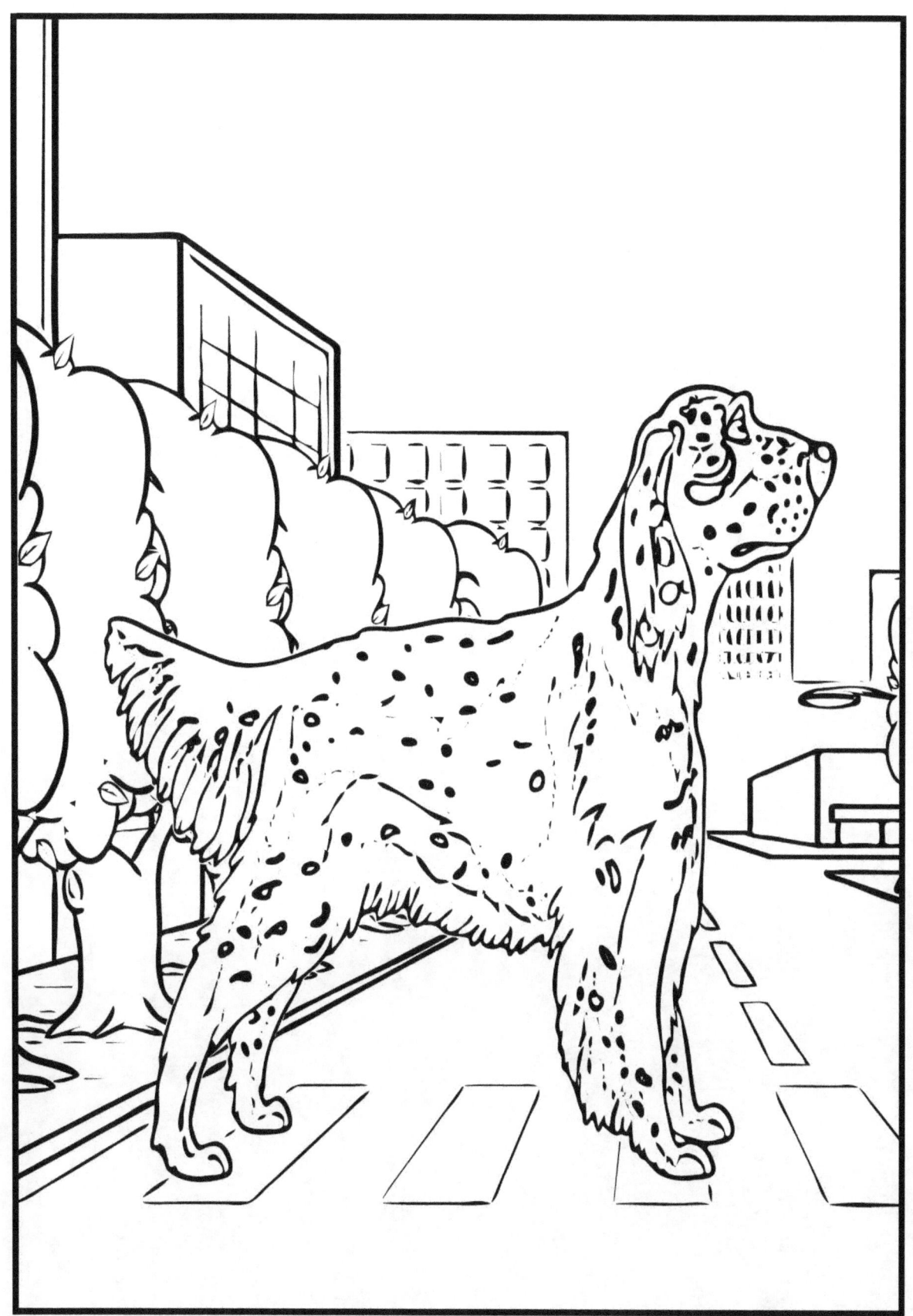

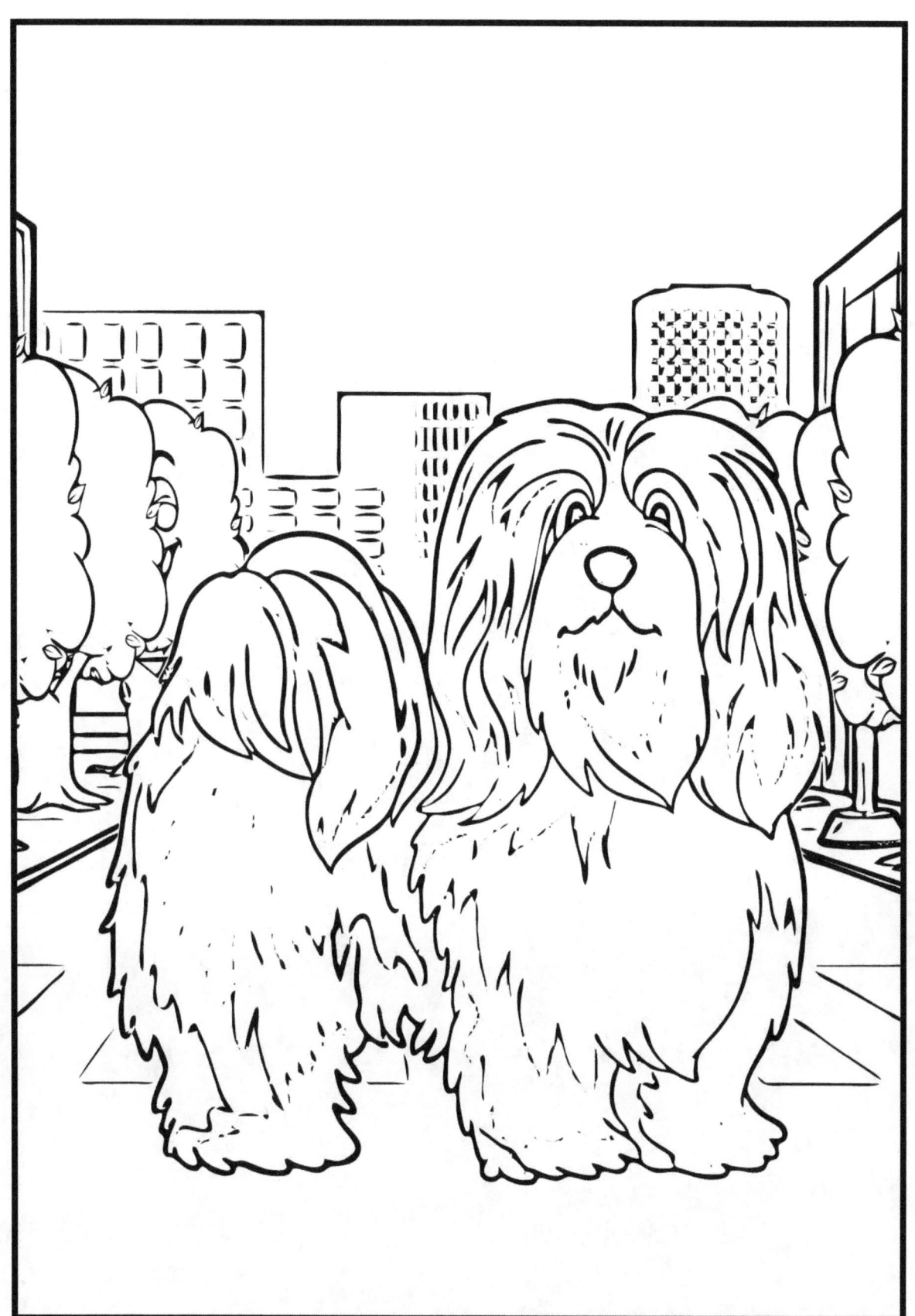

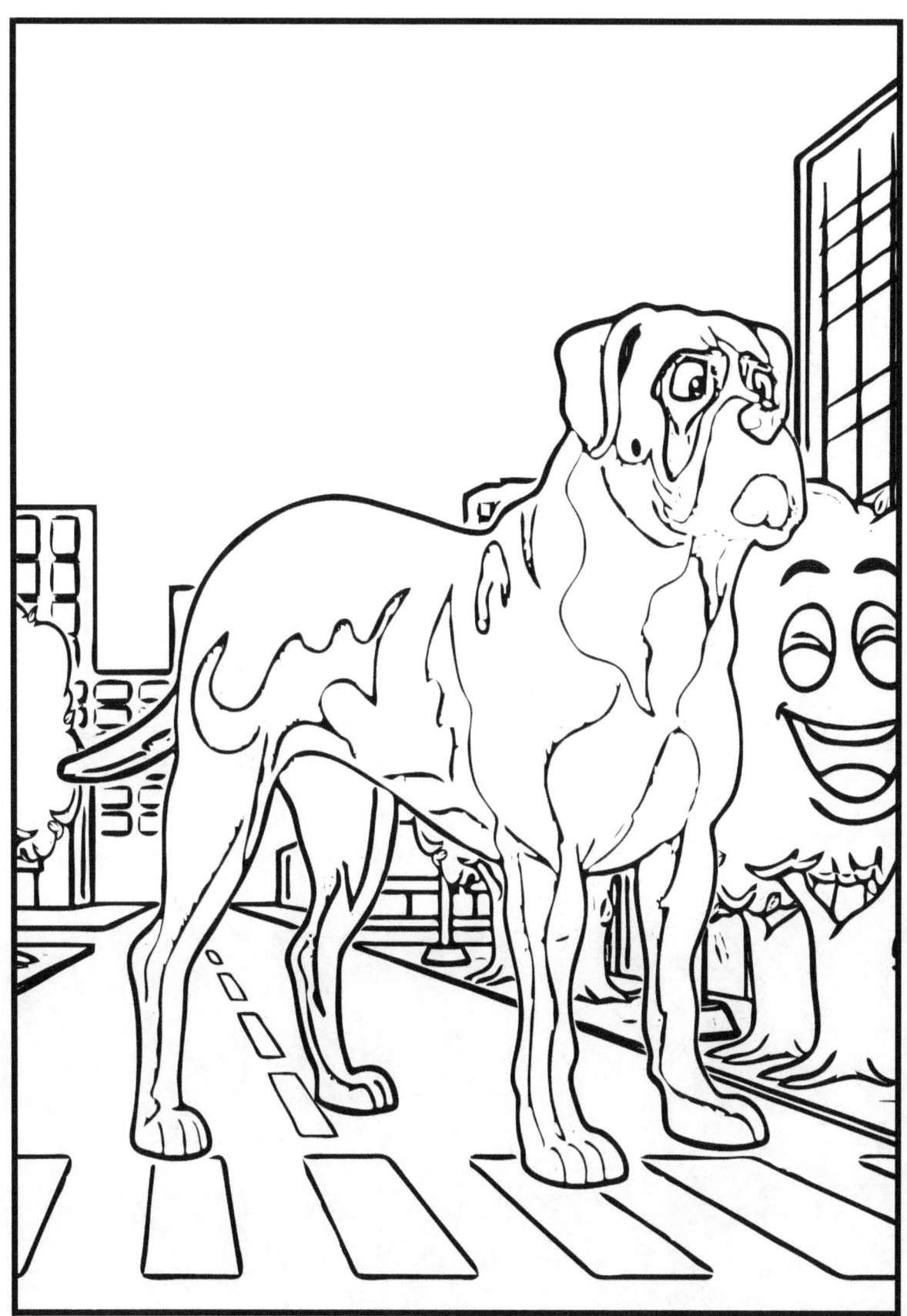

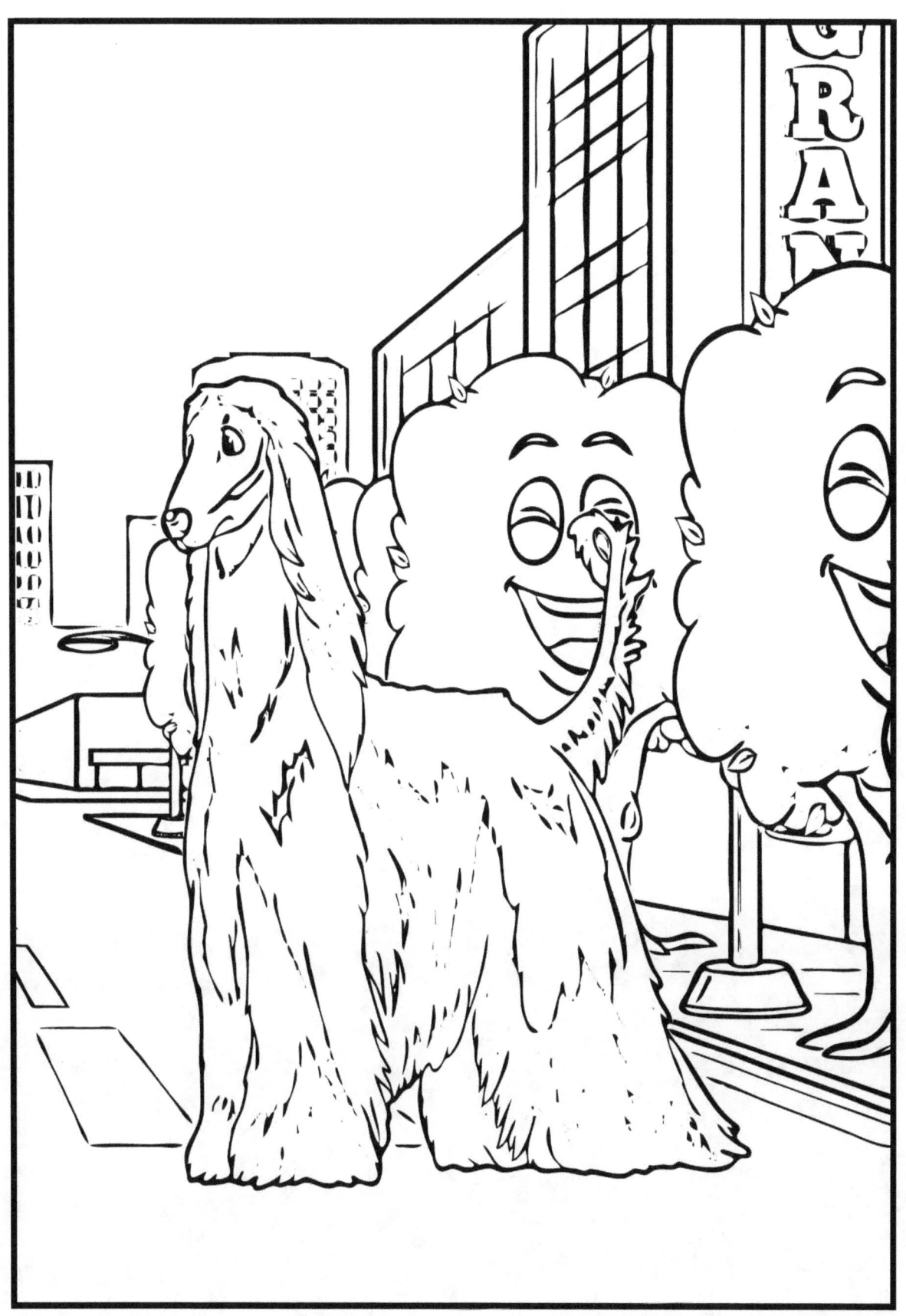

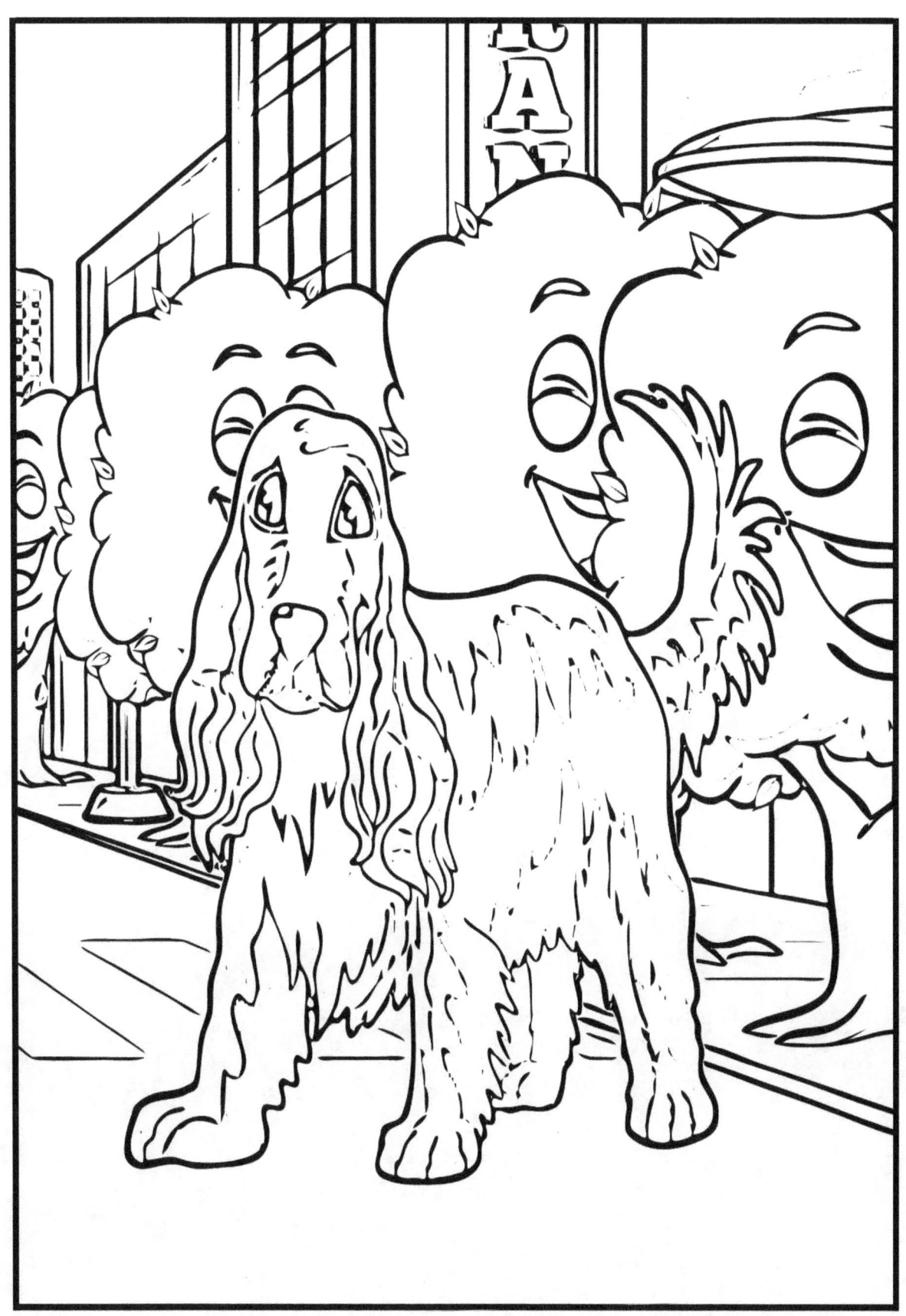

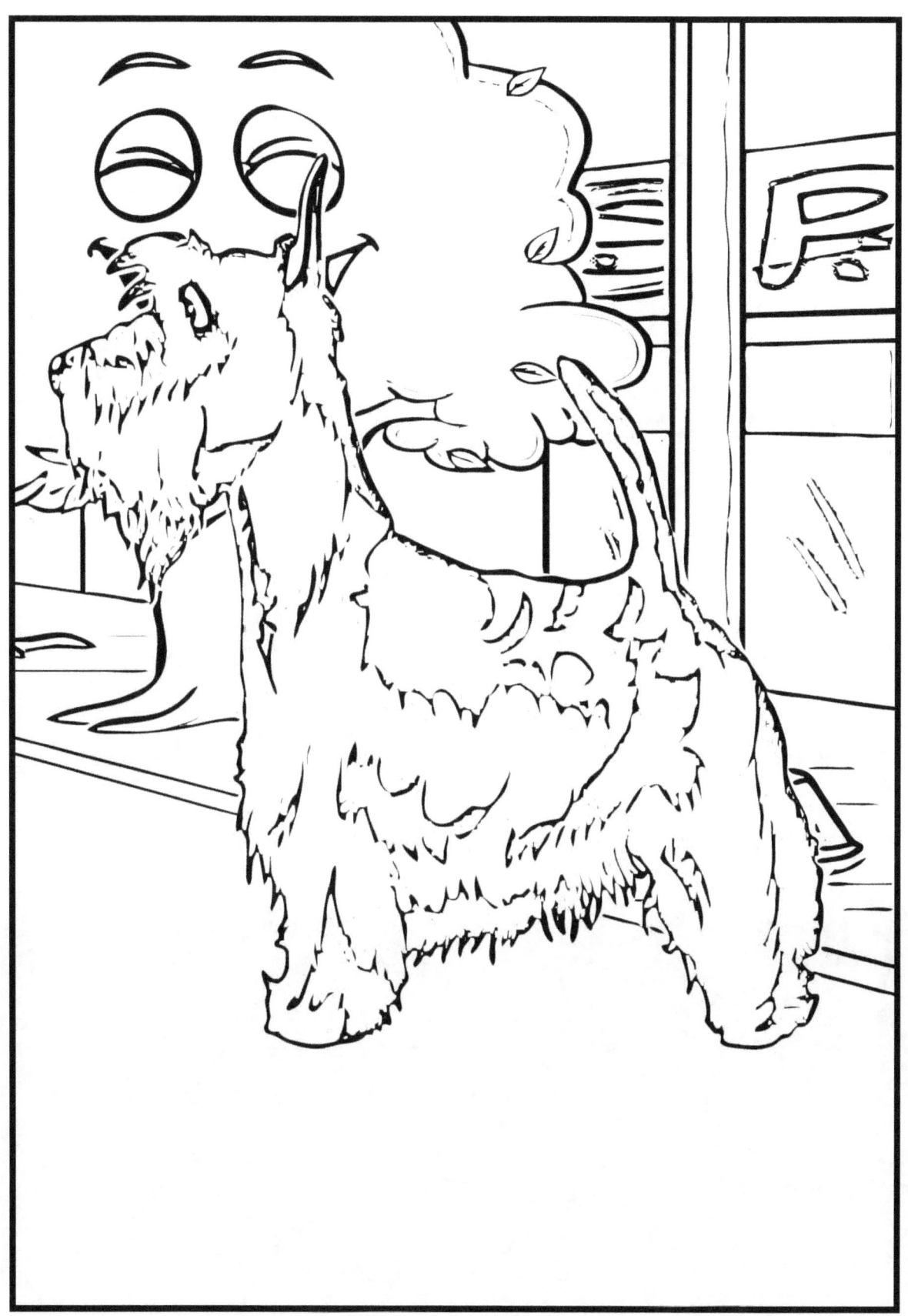

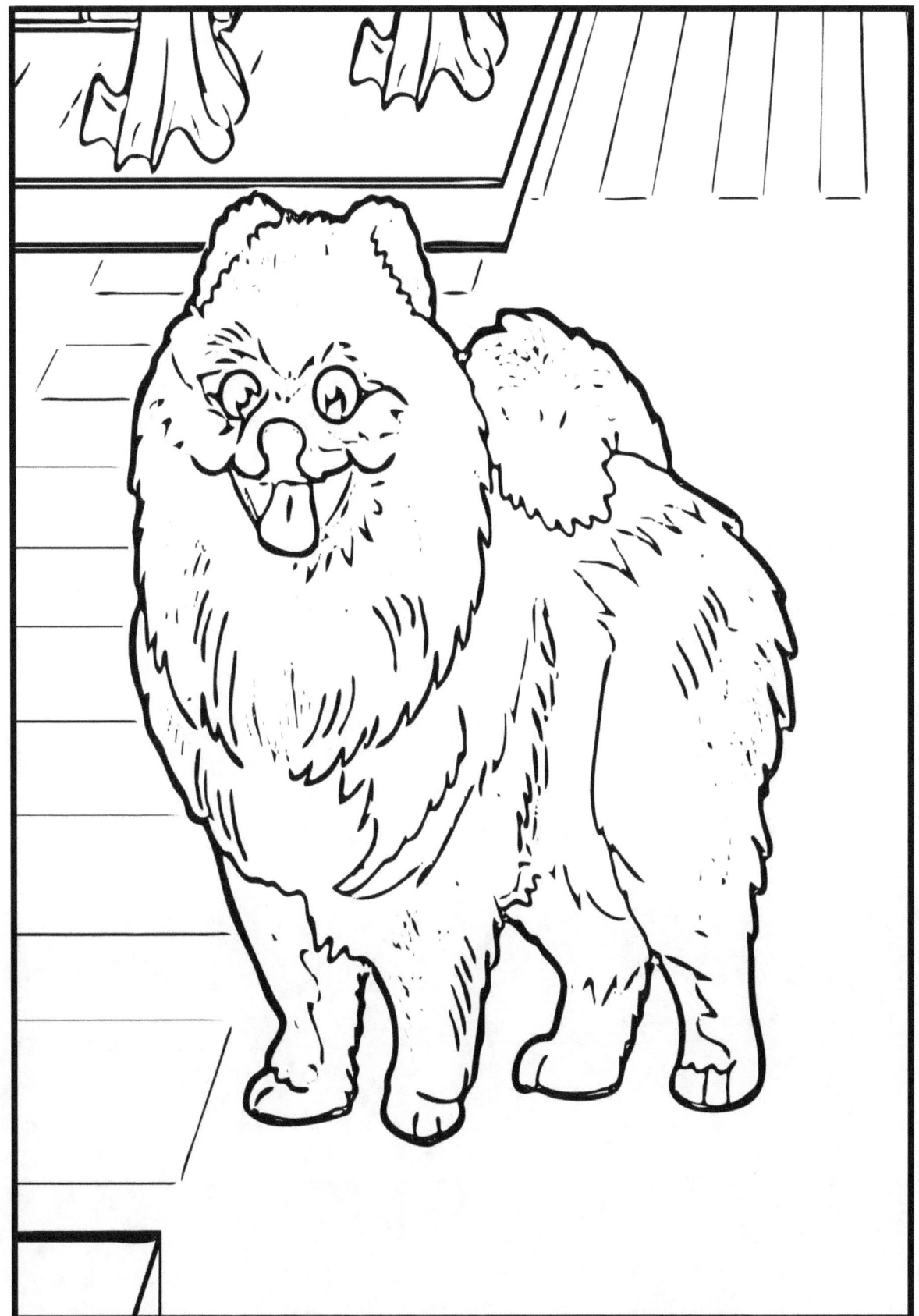

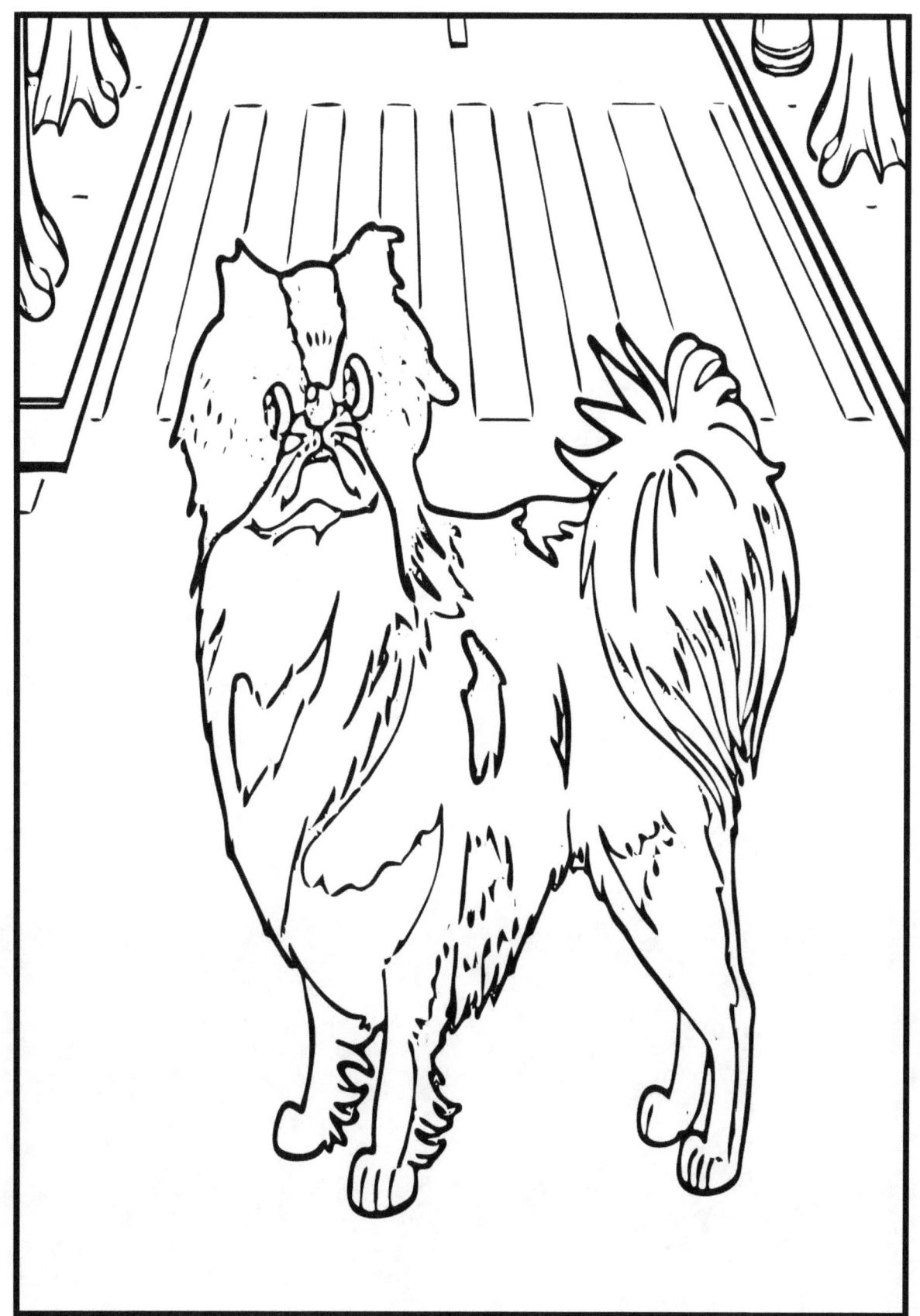

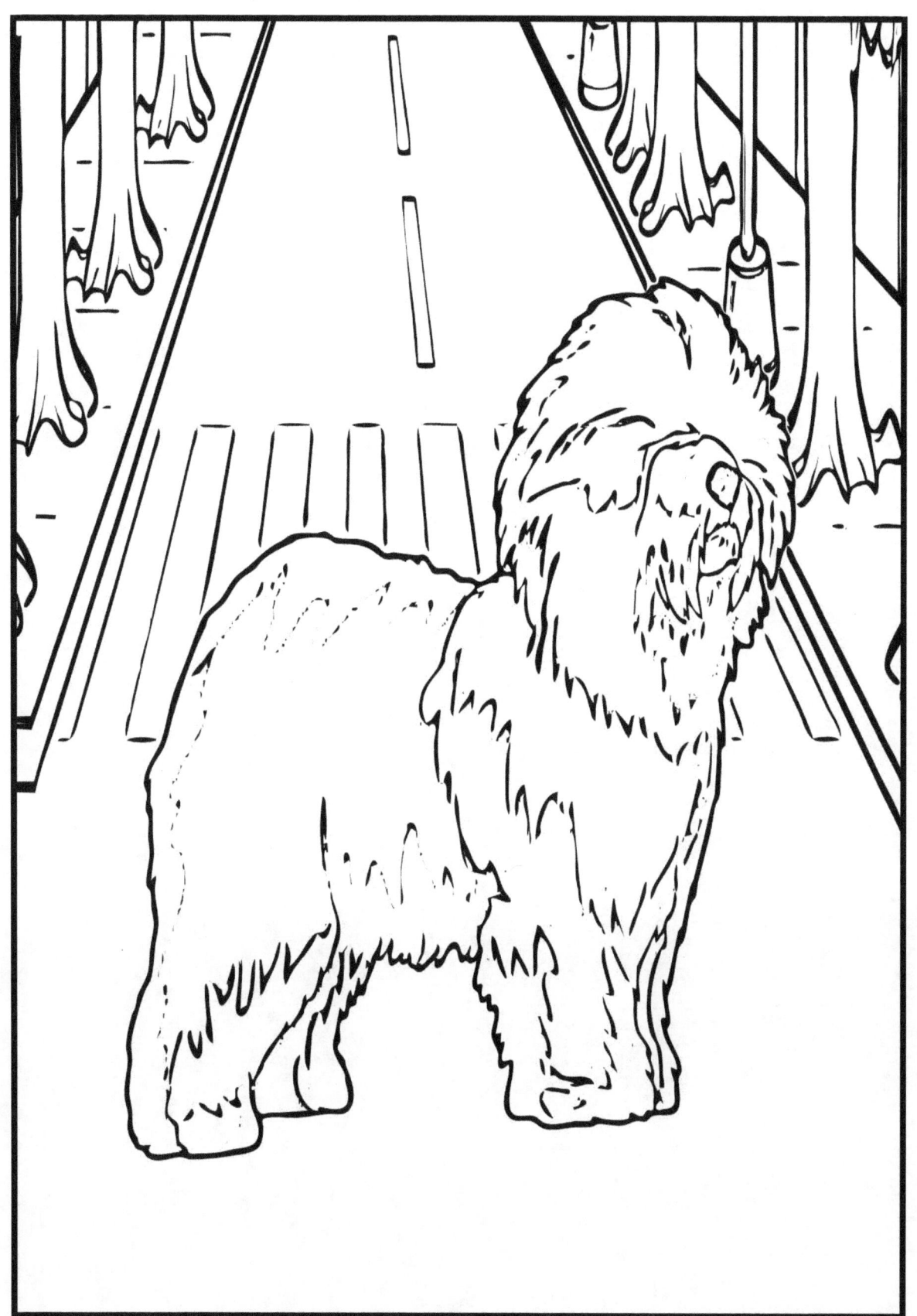

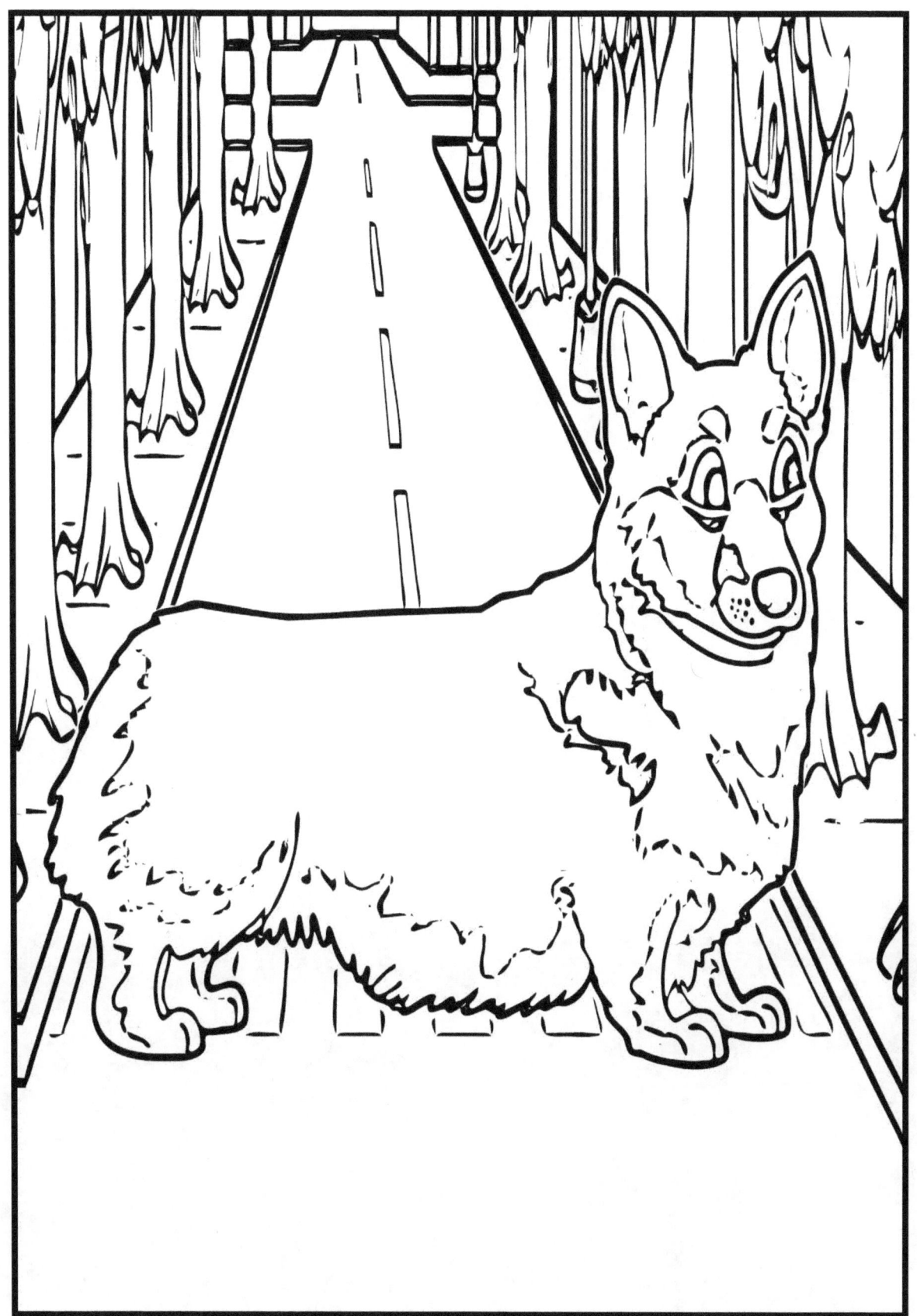

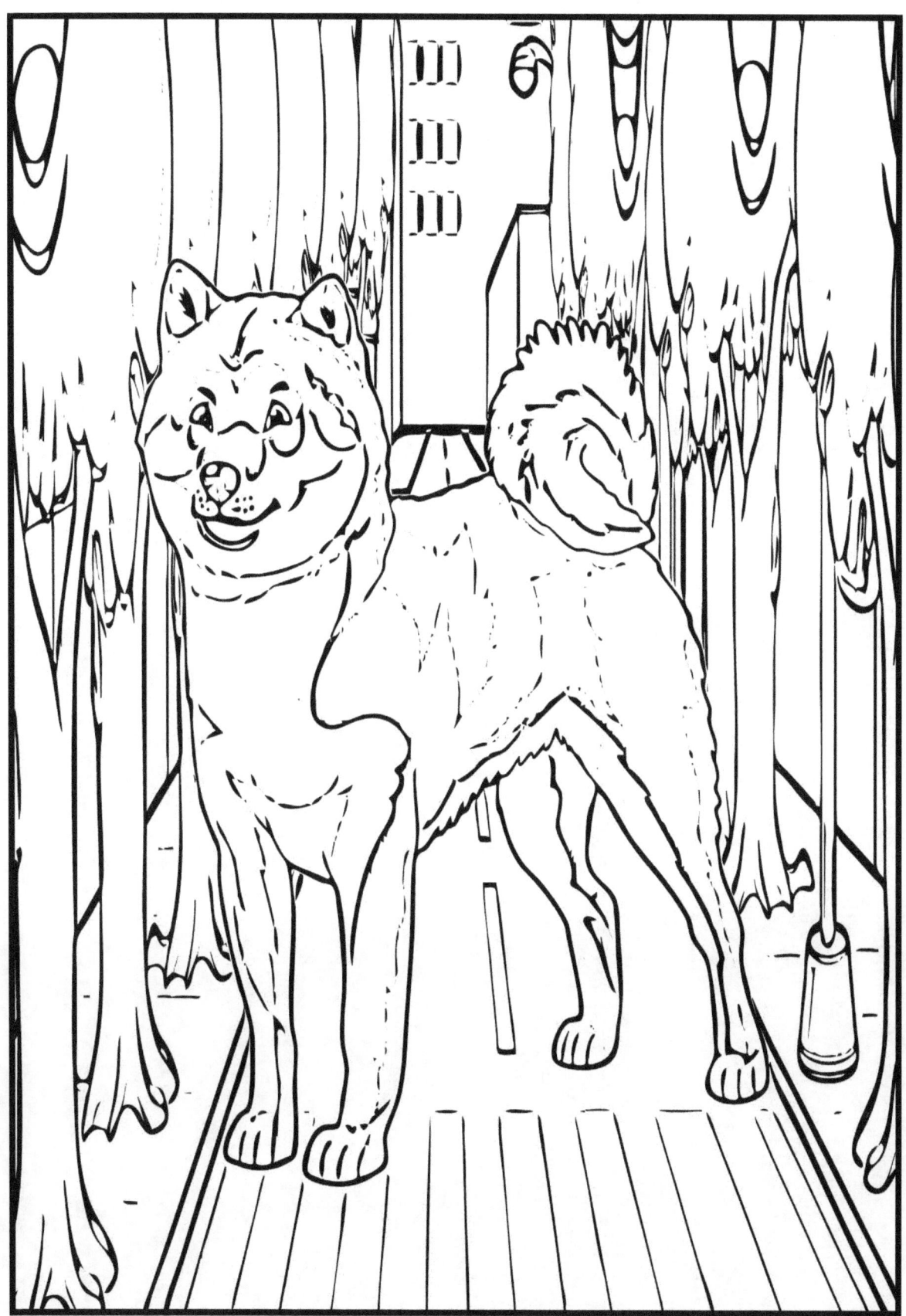

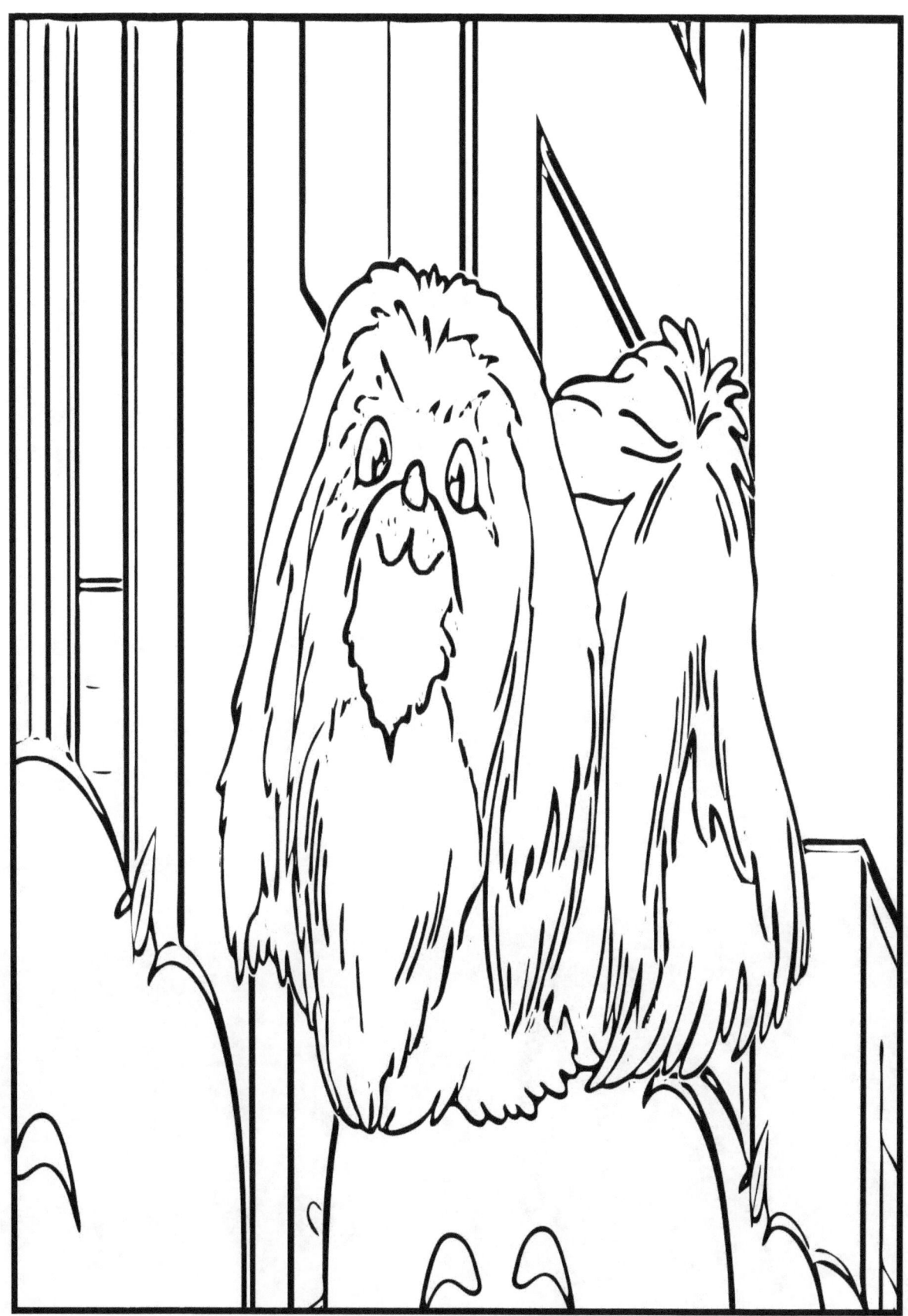

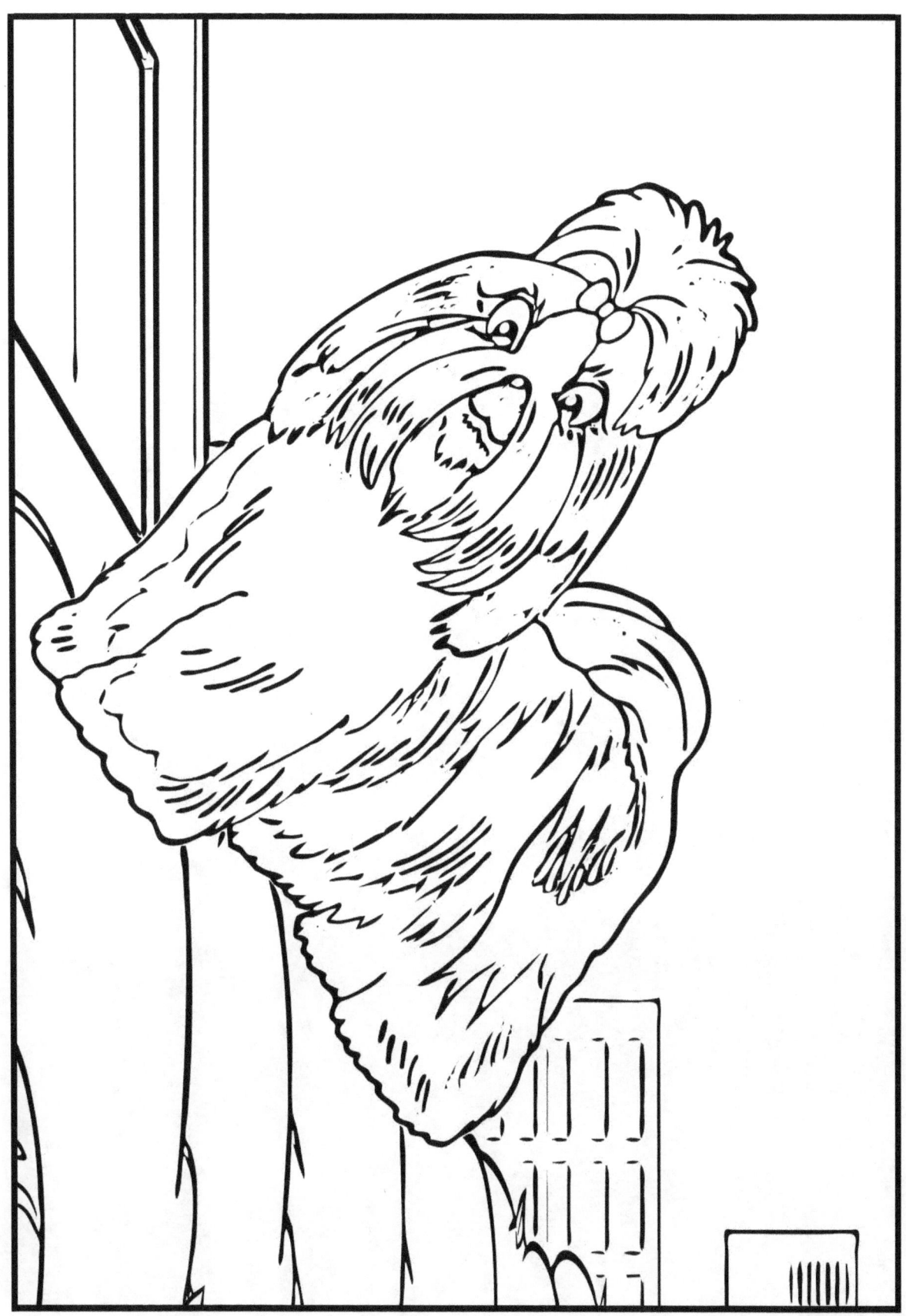

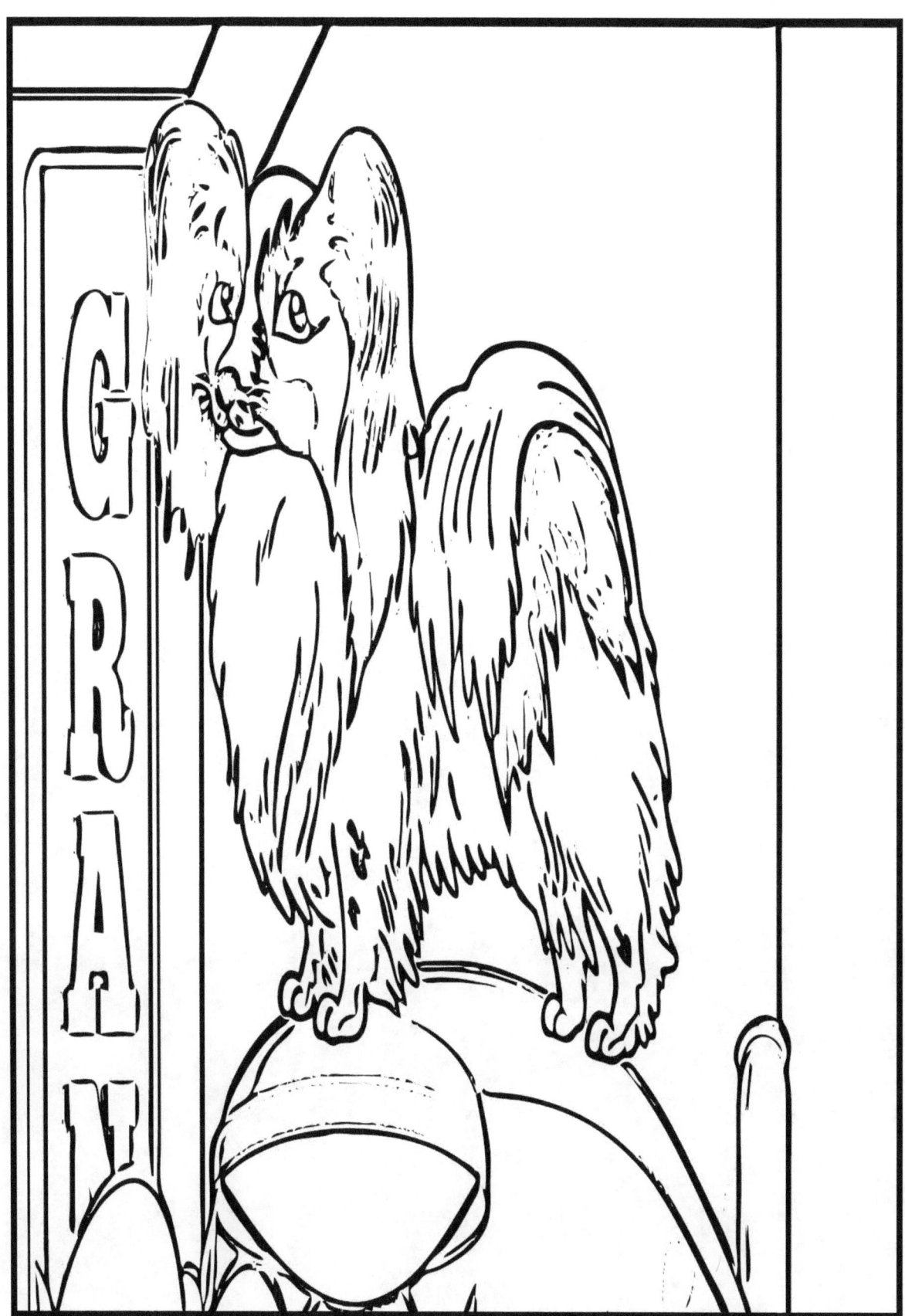

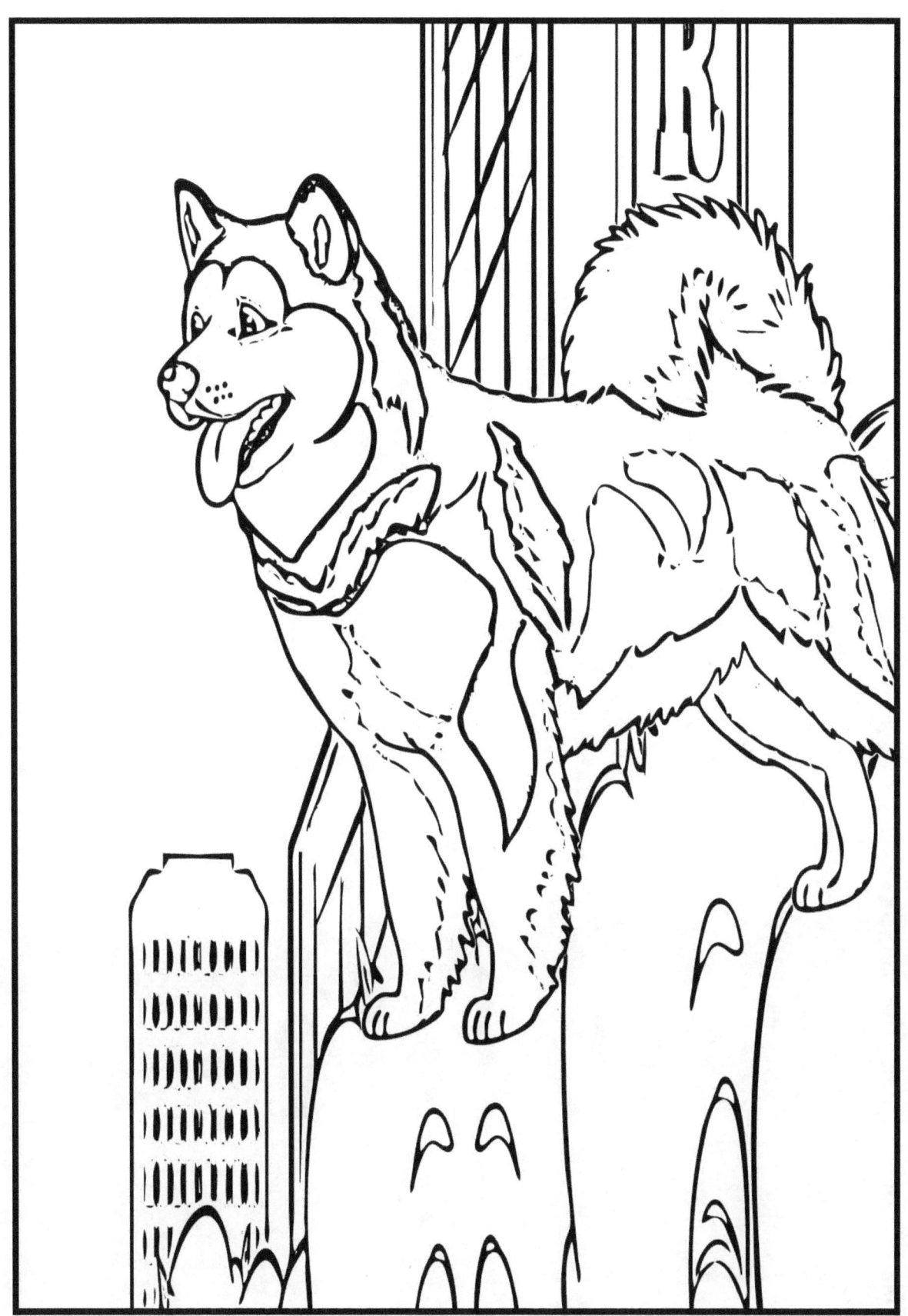

www.ingramcontent.com/pod-product-compliance
Lightning Source LLC
Chambersburg PA
CBHW080618180526
45168CB00007B/2958